RELEASE

A Study Guide for

written by
Malik Wade & Lisa D. Gray

ISBN: 9780998616728

Release

Table of Contents

ABOUT THE BOOK AND ELEVATION GUIDE

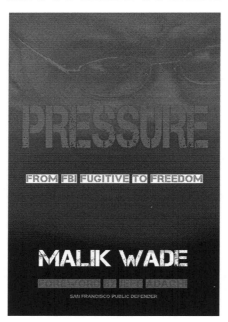

Pressure: From FBI Fugitive to Freedom tells the story of Malik Wade, a San Francisco youth who evolved into a high-level nationwide drug dealer who landed on the FBI's wanted list. The book chronicles Malik's life growing up in inner-city San Francisco, his life in Canada when he was on the run from the FBI, his conviction and fourteen-year incarceration in federal prison, and his transformation and redemption after his release.

This teaching guide, *Release*, primarily targets 15- to 24-year-old youth facing the same social challenges that Malik did as a teenager struggling to find his place in the world. While it's designed for transitional-age youth, a range of age groups will find benefit in this guide's pages. It uses hands-on, interactive activities designed to get readers to think about how they can avoid the pitfalls confronting young people living in challenged communities, particularly young men of color.

This guide integrates Freire's pedagogical concepts of conscientization, dialogue, and praxis as well as Bloom's taxonomy of learning in a series of lessons that focus on the seven core themes in the book, or what Malik describes as "The Seven Levels to Elevation."

The Seven Levels to Elevation

| Choices | Restorative Justice | Mental Health | Humility | Finding Your Place | Life Plan | Transformation |

Malik entered the federal prison system an arrogant and selfish drug dealer who only cared about making money. He soon started to transform himself into a humble, educated and enlightened man who wanted to help and heal others. Several years into his prison sentence, his desire to mentor and help those in need was solidified when he met a young man from Richmond, California named Gino. Gino had an infamous reputation and was known on the street as a "Young Gunner." Gino was serving five years on drug charges when the two met. Over the course of the next two years, Malik mentored Gino and helped him disconnect himself from his old friends and violent and unhealthy ways of thinking. His friendship with Gino is what ultimately propelled him to dedicate his life to teaching young people. Eventually, Malik committed himself to spending the remainder of his fourteen-year sentence vigorously educating himself so that he could help train and mentor more young men and women who, like Gino, come from challenged backgrounds.

ABOUT MALIK WADE

Malik Wade is a leading voice for youth in the United States and is the Executive Director of Scholastic Interest Group, a nonprofit organization and mentoring program. Every year, SIG takes fifteen young men on an all-expenses-paid college tour to universities such as UCLA, USC, Loyola Marymount, and Pepperdine. In March 2017, Malik had the mentoring experience of a lifetime when he was able to chaperone fourteen inner-city youth from  San Francisco to Accra, Ghana in Africa on a cultural pilgrimage to learn their history. Malik is the recipient of many awards. One of his crowning achievements, however, was graduating from Stanford Law School's Project ReMADE program in 2013. An in-demand speaker, he has spoken at universities including UC Berkeley and San Francisco State, as well as in correctional facilities including Dublin federal prison in California. In addition, he has facilitated workshops and training for the San Francisco Public Defender's Office and frequently speaks at different juvenile facilities throughout the state of California. He is also the CEO and founder of Pressure Publishing Company.

Release

A Message from Malik Wade

I grew up in the 1980s at the peak of the crack cocaine plague that devastated the inner cities of America. Although crack is on the decline now, other illicit drugs are still prevalent in the urban areas of America. While I grew up in a different era, I can still relate to what many youth who grow up in crime- and gang-infested neighborhoods experience today. Often, these youth come from dysfunctional family backgrounds as well. I come from a huge family that had its share of dysfunction and problems when I was growing up. The men in my family, especially my uncles on both sides, set a particular example for me to follow. On my mother's side, I had six uncles. Four have been to prison, and one of them had a shoot-out with the police and eventually died from his wounds. On my father's side, I had three uncles. One went to federal prison twice, and my other two uncles were shot and killed within one year of each other. And my father, well, he went to state and federal prison too. This pattern of incarceration is what I would eventually follow. I would ultimately be convicted on firearms charges on four separate occasions and eventually receive a fourteen-year sentence in federal prison. Going to prison is what it finally took for me to get the message and change my way of thinking.

Once I finally got out of prison after serving my fourteen-year sentence, I witnessed the same things taking place in my community that were happening before I left. The murder rate in my community was still high and rising every day, and there were young men in my own family who were intrigued and fascinated with the street life, just like I had been when I was a teenager.

When I came home and saw young men carrying pistols in their backpacks to school with their math books, and murders taking place at 9:00 in the morning just a few feet from my front door (there were more than ten murders within one mile of my doorstep during the first year after I came home from prison), I felt compelled to act and exercise many of the lessons that I had learned in prison to try to make a difference.

I wrote the book *Pressure* to send a message to the youth and my community. I wrote the book to atone and make amends for the damage that I had personally done. I wanted to apologize to my community. *Pressure* is my formal apology. If by writing my book I can save at least one life, I have done my job.

When I came home from prison, I started a nonprofit organization called Scholastic Interest Group. SIG is a mentoring program that tutors and mentors at-risk youth in my hometown of San Francisco. I wanted to develop a program that could be used as a platform to give back. For many kids in the community, SIG is the big brother, the "Big Homie" or the father figure that they never had. I appreciate my role with SIG. Running SIG and being a mentor make me proud.

It is my wish that by sharing my life lessons and experiences with the youth who read this guide, they will learn something and be inspired to be something better. I hope to spare them the trauma and negativity that I experienced as a young person. I hope that this study guide can be a blueprint used in the healing process for our youth.

Release

Background

The youth of today face significant challenges growing up. Whether they live in the inner city or the suburbs, our youth confront issues such as drug use, peer pressure to be sexually promiscuous, and problems with identity. Some of the harmful by-products of these issues are drug addiction, unwanted pregnancies, HIV, and gang/street violence. However, Malik Wade, author of the book *Pressure* and mentor to at-risk youth, is an excellent example of someone who eventually conquered these challenges. He explains how to ultimately overcome negativity with his inspirational story of survival and redemption in his book *Pressure: From FBI Fugitive to Freedom*.

Facing a life sentence at the age of 22, Malik fled the United States and stayed on the run from the FBI for the next seven years. Once arrested, he pleaded guilty and was sentenced to fourteen years in federal prison. After Malik got to prison, a change started to take place, and Malik began to read, study, and look deep into himself. As a result of the changes he made, he emerged out of the darkness of prison a man with a hope for a brighter future.

Through its writing exercises and essay discussion questions, this course and study guide will inspire readers to evaluate their own lives and will challenge them to look at things from a different perspective. As the instructor and facilitator of this course, you will embark on a path of deep self-examination and introspection with readers, and you will see how the power of writing and literature can be an instrumental tool to reach readers.

This teaching supplement will:
1. **Empower readers to understand their decision-making processes.**
2. **Inspire readers to think critically.**
3. **Assist teachers/facilitators with engaging and discussing sensitive critical issues with students.**

Teachers, group leaders, and facilitators can use this tool to guide readers to understand themselves, who they are, and where they see themselves in their communities and the world. This teaching guide addresses the principal focal points of the book and provides prompts and suggestions for teaching and learning. It also offers educational resources for teachers and instructors in the areas of social studies, political science, criminal justice, and Language Arts. It links to California Common Core, English Language Arts Standards in Reading, Listening, Writing, Speaking, and Language Progression for grades 6-12. The teachings are rooted in passages and excerpts from the book *Pressure: From FBI Fugitive to Freedom*. It offers a range of pedagogical strategies that readers can use as they navigate the challenges of their daily lives.

Writing exercises and essay questions are an integral part of this guide and have been included to help readers develop their capacity in writing and speaking. These exercises will also help them articulate their feelings about specific subject matter that applies to their own lives. Learners participate in discussions, practice critical thinking, engage in group and individual learning, and reflect on what they have learned.

Each lesson plan expands on the topics covered in the book and is designed to stimulate more profound analysis than the discussion alone could provide. Each lesson plan contains the following elements:
1. Learning Goals
2. Guiding Questions
3. Things for you as a facilitator to Ask, Tell, Explain to the group
4. Direct references to passages in the book that link to the lesson plan
5. Instructions for facilitators in red
6. Activities
7. Materials list
8. Sample handouts

"If you don't know better, you can't do better." This saying rings true and is especially appropriate when dealing with many of our youth. This guide will help readers understand their role in the community and how they can make the community stronger.

Release

The Power of Storytelling & Considerations for Delivery

Malik is a compelling writer and storyteller; Malik takes readers on an intense and never-dull journey as he tells his story. We hope that readers of Malik's book will genuinely connect with his story and will come to a better understanding of how to avoid many of the decisions that ultimately led Malik to become a fugitive for seven years and to go to federal prison with a fourteen-year sentence. We would like for Malik's story to be a blueprint to show youth how they can ultimately change and break out of the sometimes unhealthy ways of living and questionable decision-making practices that take place in some of our communities. By reading *Pressure,* we hope that readers ultimately experience and learn the power of redemption and humility.

Reading *Pressure* may stir the emotions and provoke some strong reactions from you and some of your readers. Be prepared to process and analyze some profound questions that may arise. Our youth are searching for answers to life's riddles and are still learning, yet to a significant degree, their intellectual development and understanding of life will be shaped by you, their teacher or instructor, alongside their parents. Hopefully, *Pressure* will help you put some things into proper perspective and context for them.

The students' reactions to *Pressure* will vary. Some may react with intrigue and ask a lot of questions, some may respond passive-aggressively, and others may have a difficult time processing the information altogether. This guide will assist teachers and instructors with engaging the readers around these issues and will help facilitate intense but healthy and much-needed dialogue about the students' feelings. Sometimes discussions around such serious topics evoke powerful and unpredictable responses from readers. You can assist students on understanding and processing emotions they experience in these workshops by scaffolding the lessons in several ways, which are embedded in these lesson plans.

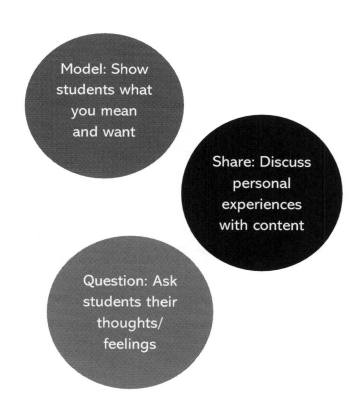

Model: Show students what you mean and want

Share: Discuss personal experiences with content

Question: Ask students their thoughts/feelings

An open and honest learning culture and environment are integral for readers to process what they have learned while reading *Pressure*. The home environment and the context of the communities they come from should always be considered. Both can have an impact on how the readers take in and process the information. Being mindful of this while using this guide should help achieve the following three goals.

You and your readers should make a mutual decision about the appropriate class activities and most relevant discussion points. These groupings should be done in the spirit of teamwork, which allows for synergistic teaching and peer-to-peer mentoring. This method allows for readers to feel more engaged and involved in their learning processes.

3 CORE GOALS FOR FACILITATORS OF THE READER'S GUIDE

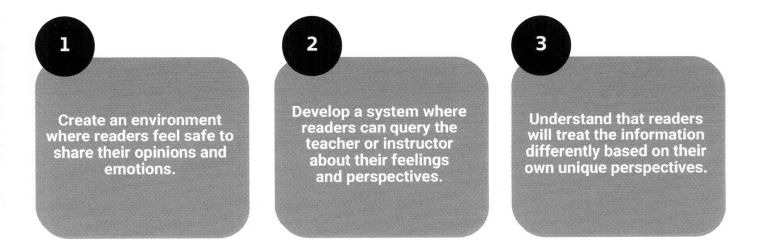

1 Create an environment where readers feel safe to share their opinions and emotions.

2 Develop a system where readers can query the teacher or instructor about their feelings and perspectives.

3 Understand that readers will treat the information differently based on their own unique perspectives.

An integral part of creating a welcoming learning environment is to use lessons and pedagogies that address a variety of learning styles. This guide utilizes pedagogies that focus on a range of styles to ensure that we meet people where they are in how they learn.

Release

Learning Culture

Learning styles are rooted in research and evidence from classrooms and educational communities. Each lesson in this guide uses at least two of the seven widely recognized learning styles. The following list of styles comes from the website *learning-styles-online.com*.

The Seven Learning Styles

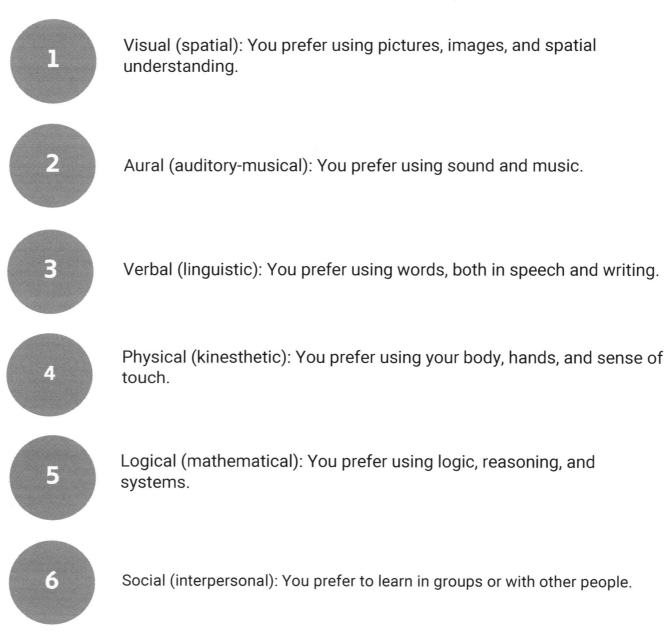

1 Visual (spatial): You prefer using pictures, images, and spatial understanding.

2 Aural (auditory-musical): You prefer using sound and music.

3 Verbal (linguistic): You prefer using words, both in speech and writing.

4 Physical (kinesthetic): You prefer using your body, hands, and sense of touch.

5 Logical (mathematical): You prefer using logic, reasoning, and systems.

6 Social (interpersonal): You prefer to learn in groups or with other people.

7 Solitary (intrapersonal): You prefer to work alone and use self-study.

Lesson Plans

"Life is a matter of choices, and every choice you make makes you."
~ John C. Maxwell

Learning Goals

Readers will learn to:

1. Understand why choices and decision making are essential and life-changing.

2. Learn the steps to decision making.

Guiding Question

What and who do you think about as you make choices about how you live your life?

From the Book

We will focus on the following text from *Pressure* as we explore how the choices we make impact our lives and the lives of those around us.

Chapter	Page Number	What motivates your decision making?
1	11	Here we learn how Malik decided to sell drugs.

Release

Choices

Tell the group: In Chapter 1, we meet Malik and learn about his lifestyle and the factors that led him to decide to become a drug dealer. We see him make choices about whether or not to step into the drug world and drug culture. He weighs his options and explores pros and cons of selling drugs to support his family. Money and survival become his motivation.

Ask the group: What motivates you in your decision making? What was the core factor driving Malik's decision to sell drugs? Why was this so important to him? What other things did he consider when making this decision? What things might he have believed that we do not see in the book?

Give them 3 minutes to think and 10 minutes to discuss these questions in small groups of three or more. No recording is necessary as there is no report back for this. This activity is designed to get them thinking.

Explain: We will spend some time exploring Malik's decision to become a drug dealer and what that led to in his life.

Activity 1: Thinking (20 - 60 mins)

1. Brainstorm a list of things that one might consider when making life-changing decisions.
2. Have the group break into small groups of three to five people and talk about the list and how these things have impacted their decision making.
3. Each group should select a talk leader, a recorder, and a timekeeper.
4. Come back together as a large group.
5. Have each small group leader report on what the group discussed.

Materials:
- Whiteboard, chalkboard, or flip chart
- Markers or chalk
- Timer or clock
- Paper
- Pens

Tell the group: Spend 10 to 30 minutes going over the steps to decision making with the group.

Steps to Good Decision Making

STEP 1: Analyze

You are confronted with a problem and need to choose how to address it. It may be as simple as what to wear today or as complex as whether or not you, like Malik, would sell drugs or engage in another activity that could compromise your freedom. Before we make the decision or choose which path to take, we must fully understand the problem. We must gather information that helps us see what is at stake.

The first step in our decision-making process is to understand and analyze the problem we face. We must ask ourselves critical questions. What do I need? What do I want? Who will be affected? What is at stake for me? What can I gain? What can I lose? What is most important? How long will it take? These are some of the questions we pose if we are to understand the scope of the problem.

STEP 2: Explore

The next step is to explore our options and weigh the pros and cons of those options. We must consider the potential outcomes of wearing sneakers as opposed to shoes or of selling drugs or not selling them. We must consider the consequences of the possible choices. For example, if I decide to skip class today, I will probably miss valuable information, and I may get called to the principal's office, get detention, or even get a suspension. My decision to skip class can also lead to me getting a poor grade, and that could mean I will have to go to credit recovery. If I decide to not go to work today, I may miss opportunities, I may get written up by my supervisor, or I may even lose my job. Every decision we make has consequences, and we must weigh the cons against the pros to see what will benefit us in the long term.

STEP 3: Decide

The final step is to make a decision. All of this can take place in an instant or over the course of hours, days, or even weeks or months. Some decisions can change the course of our lives forever. Malik's decision to sell drugs, though motivated by the desire to provide for his family, meant he put his freedom at risk and ultimately lost it as a result of this decision. When we decide, when we choose, we owe it to ourselves to do so with information and conviction because some decisions cannot be undone.

Activity 2: Doing (20 - 60 mins)

1. Have participants think of a time they made a poor decision, one where they did not thoroughly analyze and understand the problem or weigh the pros and cons.

2. Have them create a poster, poem, or story that shows what happened in the long term or aftermath as a result of that choice. The poster, poem, or story should illustrate the impact of the decision on themselves, those around them (friends, family, classmates, etc.), and their community. For example, Malik's poster might show the families that were devastated by the drugs he sold, it might show his family alone and waiting for him to return from prison, or it might show someone who experienced violence as a result of his need to protect himself while selling drugs.

3. Participants can decide if they want to share their posters and describe them to the group.

4. If possible, leave the posters in the group space to show how the decision-making process can play out and to remind participants that they can make sound decisions.

Materials:
- Poster-sized paper (11x17, flip chart or butcher paper)
- Magazines for posters
- Colored markers or crayons
- Journals (if writing)

Wrap up

Explain: Decisions can change our lives in many ways. Malik learned that he needs to use the skill of decision making and seeing all of his options if he wants to be successful outside of the world of drugs. We want you to be successful, too. Possessing the skills and tools to make decisions that lead to positive outcomes for ourselves, those around us, and our communities requires an understanding of the decision-making process. As you go through the rest of the day and week, consider how you can use the steps in the process to make good choices.

"Restorative justice says 'No, the offense affected a relationship' and what you are seeking for is to restore the relationship, to heal the relationship."
~ Desmond Tutu

Learning Goals

Readers will learn:

1. To identify times when they did wrong to a person or group of people.

2. The importance of rebuilding relationships and making restitution.

3. How restorative justice can heal communities.

Guiding Questions

What can you do to rebuild relationships broken or damaged by your words or actions? How can you help create further healing for yourself, others you have harmed with your words and actions, and your community?

From the Book

Chapter	Page Number	What can you do to rebuild relationships broken or damaged by your words or actions?
34	257 259 to 260	Here we see Malik start the process of making amends and begin to atone for the things he has done to damage his relationships with family, friends, and his community.

Release
Restorative Justice

Tell the group: Chapter 34 shows us how Malik made amends with himself and his community. We see Malik genuinely and explicitly say "I am sorry" and ask for forgiveness from his community and everyone who was affected by his criminal conduct and harmful behavior. In this chapter, he attempts to repair broken relationships. This chapter illustrates how we can use restorative justice to heal.

Explain: Restorative justice is a process that allows people and communities to find healing so that they can move forward. It re-envisions how we approach punishment and retribution in a way that allows for all parties to come together and move on from trauma induced by a person or group's words and actions. Howard Zehr created restorative justice concepts, and many justice systems around the world use them to hold one another accountable and move forward from traumatic experiences.

Show this 3-minute video titled "Restorative Justice in a Nutshell"
https://youtu.be/kfmdAJ_eNjE

Ask the group: Have you ever done something for which you are genuinely sorry or that you knew was wrong? Have your actions or words ever harmed someone in your family, one of your friends, or your community?

Activity 1: Thinking (10 mins)
Give them 10 minutes to think about these questions and have them use the *Restorative Justice Worksheet* to list two or more times they caused harm to themselves, their family, friends, or the community in the appropriate sections of the sheet.

Explain: There are three steps in the restorative justice process. We will spend the next 45 minutes focusing on the levels and how you can use them in your life. (Use handout *The Steps to Achieving Restorative Justice*).

Materials:
- Handouts
- Pens/pencils

Sample Handout

Restorative Justice Worksheet

I'm sorry for when I...	Who did my actions hurt? (Myself, my family, my friends, my community?)	How were my actions hurtful?

Release

Restorative Justice

The Steps to Achieving Restorative Justice

 Recognize that you have done wrong. Before you can apologize for the harm you caused, you must admit to yourself and others that you hurt them in some way. You have to acknowledge the things you did without making excuses for why you did them.

 Issue an apology and seek forgiveness. Once you have admitted the wrong you have done and the harm you have caused, you must find a way to apologize. You can also ask those you have harmed to forgive you for what you have done to them. Your apology can take many forms. Malik wrote a letter; every apology is different, but all apologies should be three things.

3 THINGS EVERY APOLOGY SHOULD BE

1 Sincere: Make it come from the heart. Take time to think about it. Get clear on what you want to say and how you want to say it.

2 Direct: Don't be passive-aggressive. Address those whom you have harmed.

3 Specific: Address specific situations and instances, and be clear about the reasons you are remorseful for your actions or words.

 Demonstrate through actions that you are sorry. The final step speaks to making restitution for the things you have done. This too can take many forms. You could fix the things you broke or volunteer at a place representative of the person or place you harmed (for example, a senior center or a youth organization). You could pay for the things you stole or broke. The key to real restorative justice is making things right with yourself and those impacted by your words/actions and also changing your behavior.

Activity 2: Doing

Have the group go back to their lists of the people and communities they have harmed and pick one to focus on for this exercise. You can choose to do one or both of these activities, and they can occur over one or more sessions:

1. (45 - 90 mins) Apologize to the person, people, or community they selected. This apology can take any form. They, like Malik, can write a letter; they can create a song or poem; they can come up with an artistic idea; or they can make a verbal apology.

2. (2 - 4 weeks) Come up with a 5-point written plan for giving back. This plan can take many forms (verbal, written, video, audio, visual) and giving back can take place at one of several levels:

1. Personal - themselves or another person
2. Family
3. Community

Materials:

- Paper
- Magazines
- Markers
- Video cameras
- Cameras
- Computers
- Scissors
- Pens/pencils

Wrap Up

Explain: Restorative justice helped the people of South Africa begin to heal after years of racial tension and oppression. Prisons and schools are adopting restorative justice ideas and practices and changing how they approach making restitution for crimes and creating disciplinary actions. As Malik says at the beginning of Chapter 34, the goal of restorative justice in the Seven Levels of Elevation is for you as readers to learn to make an apology, seek forgiveness, and heal damaged relationships so that you and those you have harmed can move forward.

Release
Mental Health

"There are wounds that never show on the body that are deeper and more hurtful than anything that bleeds."
~ *Laurell K. Hamilton,* Mistral's Kiss

Learning Goals

Readers will learn to:

1. Understand what mental health is and why it is essential to being a healthy person.
2. Recognize when they or someone they know may need support.
3. Know how and where they can find help.
4. Develop empathy, compassion, and understanding for those experiencing mental health challenges.

Guiding Question

How do you cope with fear, sadness, depression, stress, and trying times?

From the Book

Throughout the book we see Malik grapple with stress and fear as he navigates his life as a drug dealer and fugitive. We learn how not having a father and being a father impacted his perception of himself. Malik struggles with depression and rationalizing his actions. We see this in the following passages.

From the Book (con't)

Chapter	Page Number	How do you cope with fear, sadness, depression, stress, and trying times?
4	27	This chapter talks about the mental trauma and feelings of inadequacy that Malik and other guys in his neighborhood occasionally experienced by not having a consistent father figure in their lives. It also deals with the trauma that they caused by not being consistent fathers in the lives of their children.
9	59	This chapter talks about the stress, anxiety, and depression that he experienced by being a fugitive from the FBI.
7	45	The very first paragraph describes Malik's state of mind and emotions right after being told that he is facing a life sentence in federal prison.
10	67	"Frustrations, fears, and failures. Emotional roller coaster rides. Swinging back and forth on the brink of the breaking point. Persistent pressure that could burst a pipe. Tapping into my deepest emotions. Getting in tune with all five senses. Thoughts of self-doubt and uncertainty about my future. The steady whisper of negative self-talk."

Tell the group: Good mental health is critical to being a healthy person. All too often, we do not think or talk about our mental state and how it can impact our decision making and how we see ourselves. We each owe it to ourselves, our families, and our communities to bring our best selves as often as we can. We must seek out people to share our stories with—people who can give us support and help us find ways to cope. We all struggle with negative self-talk, doubt, and feelings of inadequacy; we all experience times when life seems too big and too hard. The goal is to attain a sense of well-being, a state of happiness that occurs more often than a sense of being weighed down. The challenge is in finding the people and places that can help us navigate these trying times.

Explain: One thing we can do to understand how we feel and if we should seek support is to make a self-assessment of our feelings about our lives. We are going to explore some of the times we have felt

Release
Mental Health

sad, fearful, alone, or stressed out and explore some resources we can use to handle tough situations as well as create a strategy for well-being.

Resources:
- http://www.mentalhealthamerica.net/deal-better-hard-times
- https://classroommentalhealth.org/in-class/thoughts/

Ask the group: When have you felt stressed, sad, depressed, or overwhelmed? What did you do about it? How did you cope?

Explain: We can think of how we cope with situations that are hard to deal with as a cycle. Something happens, we have thoughts about it, these thoughts bring out feelings, and these feelings lead us to do things that we hope or think will make us feel better.

Activity 1: Thinking (10 mins)
Have the group list a time they felt
- stressed
- depressed
- happy
- sad
- overwhelmed

For each instance, have them describe how they coped with that situation.

Materials:
- Handouts
- Pens/pencils

Sample Handout

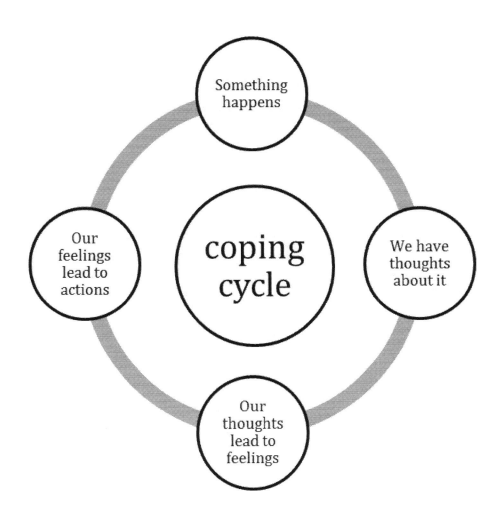

Release

Mental Health

Sample Handout

A time I felt stressed was when	Thoughts I had about this situation were	I dealt with the feelings by
A time I felt depressed was when	Thoughts I had about this situation were	I dealt with the feelings by
A time I felt happy was when	Thoughts I had about this situation were	I dealt with the feelings by
A time I felt sad was when	Thoughts I had about this situation were	I dealt with the feelings by
A time I felt overwhelmed was when	Thoughts I had about this situation were	I dealt with the feelings by

Explain: Review some of the thoughts you had. Are they things you think for yourself or because other people or groups have told you, directly or indirectly, to feel that way? Lots of times our thoughts about specific situations spring from things we have heard from friends, parents, teachers, family members, people in groups we belong to, and society. The trick is to know that the thoughts you're having and that drive your bad feelings come not from you but the messages you received from outside sources.

For example, someone calls you a name. You think, "Maybe they're right," "I should lose weight," "I am not good enough," "Why try? I'm going to fail anyway." These negative thoughts come not from you but from what others have told you. We must learn to turn off that tape and switch to a new one so that we can change our feelings and behaviors.

We teach our brains how we will handle situations. The cycle we create when something bad, stressful, or sad happens begins when we are children. We can change the cycle if we want. We have to learn new ways of coping and understand that there is nothing wrong with seeking help. Just like we can learn to make more meaningful choices, we can learn how to cope with hard situations.

Activity 2: Doing (90 mins)

Set up stations around the room by creating signs that you hang on the wall or in a place where they are visible to all. Tell the group that they are going to explore some things we can do when we are going through hard times.

> Station 1: Breathing exercises
> Station 2: Meditation exercise
> Station 3: Yoga exercise
> Station 4: Writing exercise

Allow readers to spend time at each location engaging in different coping strategies. You can invite guests in to lead the practices or provide directions and have them do the activities self-directed. They should try the activity at each station.

Materials:

- Station signs
- Instructions for stations

Activity 3: Doing (60 - 90 mins)

In small groups of at least three, have them identify and discuss three coping mechanisms they can explore and use. Have one person act as a leader, one act as a recorder, and one act as a timekeeper. Come back to a large group and share. Have them complete their *Personal Coping Strategy* using the handout.

Materials:

- Handouts
- Paper and pens/pencils

Mental Health

> Sample Handout

Coping Strategies

Things I can do when I feel:

Sad

1.

2.

3.

I can talk to

I can go to

Depressed

1.

2.

3.

I can talk to

I can go to

Angry

1.

2.

3.

I can talk to

I can go to

Stressed

1.

2.

3.

I can talk to

I can go to

Overwhelmed

1.

2.

3.

I can talk to

I can go to

Confused

1.

2.

3.

I can talk to

I can go to

Wrap Up

Explain: This is a process. Developing strong coping skills can take time. We must be mindful of this and give ourselves room to grow into new ways of dealing with hard situations. The key is not to be afraid to do something different, and not to be scared to seek help from friends, family, and mental health professionals.

Release

Humility

"Humility is the solid foundation of all virtues."
~ Confucius

Learning Goals

Readers will learn:

1. To identify humility.
2. How to be humble.

Guiding Question

How can humility and being humble keep you focused on attaining your goals?

Chapter	Page Number	How can humility and being humble keep you focused on attaining your goals?
22	155	Malik's parole officer challenges him by expecting him to return to his house in five minutes when the journey from her office takes ten. She confronts him when he arrives, and he writes, "Humility failed me and I blurted out, I just left your office fifteen minutes ago." This statement and the way he conveyed it could cost him his freedom.

Ask the group: What is humility to you? Have them shout out answers and record them in a place where everyone can see them.

Tell the group: Humility is the opposite of pride. When we practice humility, we not only put others first, but we are mindful of how our words and actions can impact the outcomes we want to achieve. We will spend some time today exploring the idea of humility and how it can make us better people and allow us to reach our goals. Being humble does not mean you cannot have pride in yourself and your work. It does mean that you do not listen to your ego and see yourself as better than others. It means that you do not allow pride to keep you from getting down in the mud with others while you work together to achieve a goal. Humility allows you to accept criticism, listen, and be your best self.

Activity 1: Thinking (10 mins)

Ask the group: What does humility look like?

Explain: In the movie *Cinderella Man*, Jim Braddock loses his career as a prizefighter. He was one of the best, and he and his family were wealthy from his winnings. Then he breaks his hand in the ring. Braddock and his family go from riches to rags, and at one point he can't pay the utility bill and must humble himself and ask the men who saw him as a boxing god for money.

Show the clip.

Resource:
http://www.wingclips.com/movie-clips/cinderella-man/asking-for-money

Then:
- Break the group into small groups of three to seven.
- Each group should have a leader, a recorder, and a presenter.
- Write the following questions where everyone can see them.
- Have the group answer the questions.
- Come back together and have each presenter tell how they answered the questions.

Ask the group:
- What showed you that Braddock was humble?
- Do you think this was hard for him? Why or why not?

Materials:
- Projector/screen
- Computer
- Paper and pens/pencils

Release
Humility

Tell the group: As I said earlier, pride is the opposite of humility, but what does that mean? Review the handout with the group.

Materials:
- Handouts
- Pens/pencils

> Sample Handout

Pride vs. Humility

PRIDE	HUMILITY
Knows it all	Seeks to learn
Does it alone	Asks for help
Talks to hear itself	Listens to understand others
Sees others' differences as problems	Sees others' differences as assets
Judges	Accepts
Criticizes	Compliments
Thinks it is perfect	Knows it is imperfect
Does not see fault in itself	Questions itself
Does not do for others	Assists others in need
Unbendable	Bends
Never apologizes	Always apologizes
Goes off	Sucks it up
Expects recognition	Does not need recognition

Humility

Activity 2: Doing (60 - 90 mins)

Tell the group: One way to practice being humble is to compliment others and show/tell them that you appreciate them and why. Let's practice that.

- Have the group stand in a circle.
- Ask one person to go to the middle of the circle.
- Three people tell the person in the middle one thing they appreciate about him or her.
- Continue until everyone has had a chance to be in the center.
- Go back to the large group and discuss how it felt to give and get compliments.
- Challenge the group to give at least one compliment to someone every day.

Materials:
- None

Activity 3: Doing (30 mins) (*NOTE: This exercise requires two sessions.*)

Tell the group: Another way to practice being humble is to do something good for someone else.

- Explain that each of them will do three "random acts of kindness" in the next week.
- Tell them that a random act of kindness is when you do something nice for someone without expecting any thanks or recognition.

Give them examples:
- Buy a cup of coffee for the person behind you in line.
- Hand out an envelope with $5 in it to a stranger.
- Give flowers or candy to random people on the street.
- Help someone with their homework.
- In the next session, spend 10 to 15 minutes talking about how it felt to do something good for someone without being asked or expecting recognition for it.

Materials:
- None

Wrap Up

Tell the group: One way to practice humility is to ask for help, as The Cinderella Man did. Another is to give compliments to people when they deserve them. You can also take a good look in the mirror and accept your imperfections. Maybe you're not the best at something. Humility allows us to be okay with that. You can also question yourself in situations when you make hard choices. Humility allows you to be a good team player and leader. Humility also allows you to make compromises when you find yourself at an impasse with someone or another group. Humble people know when to make an apology, and when things go wrong, they can "suck it up" and move on. They don't feel the need to prove themselves, and they don't get stuck in the need to be right because they know it is all right to be wrong. Malik learned the value of humility in achieving his goal to stay free. He learned how to talk to people and when to bend. He began to understand that to heal, he needed to apologize to those he had wronged. This is what we want for you.

Release
Finding Your Place

"The mystery of human existence lies not in just staying alive, but in finding something to live for."
~ *Fyodor Dostoyevsky*, The Brothers Karamazov

Learning Goals

Readers will learn to:

1. Begin answering the question, "Who Am I?"
2. Understand their purpose in life.

Guiding Questions

Who am I? And why am I here?

From the Book

Chapter	Page Number	Who am I? And why am I here?
15	109	Malik asks himself questions that focus on his understanding of who he is as a person. He seeks the answer to the question, "Why are you here on this earth?" These are fundamental questions that we all must ask ourselves.
16	117	The very last line of this chapter says, "In prison, as in the outside world, you have to be a strategic thinker." It illustrates the idea that no matter where you find yourself, you must always be able to "Figure It Out."
20	137	Here Malik explores religion vs. spirituality and how these concepts can affect your understanding of your place in the world. It can help determine how you define your life goals, values, and purpose.

Tell the group: One of the things that Malik grapples with in the book is understanding his place in the world. He seeks to answer fundamental questions about his existence; he wants to make sense of it all. He also finds that to survive, he must develop his skills as a critical thinker, and that these critical thinking skills can help him in answering these questions.

Ask the group: What are you good at and what do you like to do?

Activity 1: Thinking (10 mins)

Explain: In this exercise, you will explore the question, "Who Am I?" and begin to formulate answers that help you claim your place in the world.

Everyone is good at something. We all have things that we love to do even if we don't know how to do them all that well. In the next seven minutes, you will think about the things you like to do and the things you hate doing, as well as the things at which you are expert. These can be anything. No rules, no boundaries, no judgments.

You will use the handout to make three lists:
- Things I Like Doing
- Things I Hate Doing
- Things at Which I Am an Expert

Release

Finding Your Place

Sample Handout

Things I Like Doing	Things I Hate Doing	Things at Which I Am an Expert
Dancing	Geometry	Snapchat videos
Reading comics	Reading books	Doodling and drawing
Cooking	Talking in front of people	Making pizza

Activity 2: Thinking (15 - 30 mins)

Explain: One of the critical factors that helps us to answer these fundamental questions is our values system. Values serve as the foundation for how we choose to live our lives. Think of a compass and how it can guide you from one place to another. Your values act as your moral compass, and they guide you as you move from situation to situation. They point you in the right direction when you are making decisions, large and small. We learn our values from cues we get from the world around us.

Ask the group: "Who teaches us our values?" and have them shout out answers as you write them on the board or on a piece of butcher paper on the wall. Spend a few minutes talking about the responses.

Materials:
- Chalkboard, whiteboard, or paper hung on the wall

Activity 3: Thinking (10 - 20 mins)
Guided Meditation

Ask the group to get comfortable in the space. You can do this exercise in quiet or with background music. You will ask the group to close their eyes and then lead them in a three-minute group breathing exercise. Wait three minutes and let the group settle. You will ask a question and give the group two to three minutes to reflect before moving on to the next question in the list.

1. *When have you felt happiest? Think of a time when you felt pride in an accomplishment.*
2. *What about those times gave you the feelings that come along with pride in doing well—happiness, joy, etc.?*
3. *When have you felt regret about a decision you made? Think of the times you felt frustrated, unfulfilled, empty, or annoyed. These are signs that your values are out of sync with decisions you're making or with those around you.*
4. *What activities do you find challenging and fulfilling? What activities make you lose track of time?*
5. *Who do you look up to? What do you admire about them? These are people you find inspirational, who embody qualities or lead a lifestyle you aspire to.*

Materials:
- Instrumental music to play in background

Activity 4: Doing (60 - 120 mins)
My Values

Use the list of values from the *Core Values List* handout to create flashcards. Make one card per value. Then create a set of value

Release
Finding Your Place

cards for each reader/participant. Place the decks of value cards into envelopes or boxes for each reader/participant. Tell participants to open their envelopes.

Next, you will:

- Give them 20 minutes to review the cards and explore their meanings using: the internet, group discussion, dictionaries.
- After 20 minutes, tell them to pick ten values that they believe characterize their values system. Tell the group to put the values they chose back into the envelope.
- Tell the group to set aside the other cards.
- Give the group 15 minutes to decorate their envelopes using materials such as crayons, markers, glitter, glue sticks, old magazines, photos, etc.
- Now tell them to pick ten more values from the cards they set aside that also characterize their values systems. Tell them to add these to their envelopes.
- Give them 15 minutes to add their names to their values envelopes and do additional decorating if they'd like.
- Tell them to pick five more values from their remaining cards that characterize their values systems.
- Have them put these five values into their envelopes. Collect the cards that they do not choose.

Ask the group: How did you feel while doing this exercise? What did you learn about yourself and how you want to live your life? Did you have a difficult time narrowing down your top values? Which round was easiest to choose? Why?

Materials:

- Value cards
- Envelopes
- Materials for decorating the envelopes, such as crayons, markers, glitter, glue sticks, old magazines, photos, etc.

Use this list to create your value cards for the activity.

Core Values List

- Authenticity
- Achievement
- Adventure
- Authority
- Autonomy
- Balance
- Beauty
- Boldness
- Compassion
- Challenge
- Citizenship
- Community
- Competency
- Contribution
- Creativity
- Curiosity
- Determination
- Fairness
- Faith
- Fame
- Friendships
- Fun
- Growth
- Happiness
- Honesty
- Humor

- Influence
- Inner Harmony
- Justice
- Kindness
- Knowledge
- Leadership
- Learning
- Love
- Loyalty
- Meaningful Work
- Openness
- Optimism
- Peace
- Pleasure
- Poise
- Popularity
- Recognition
- Religion
- Reputation
- Respect
- Responsibility
- Security
- Self-Respect
- Service
- Spirituality
- Stability

- Success
- Status
- Trustworthiness
- Wealth
- Wisdom

Release
Finding Your Place

Activity 3: Doing (60 - 120 mins)
My Values in Action

Have the group take 15 to 20 minutes to re-view the values in their envelopes.

Explain: Now we are going to see how we al-ready live our values and how we can use our values to guide our actions.

Tell the group: Take your top five values and make a list of three things you have done in the past two weeks that show how you used each value. Maybe you decided to help a class-mate; perhaps you handed in your homework, did the dishes, or took your kid brother to bas-ketball practice.

Now think of three things you did without lis-tening to your values system. Maybe you watched television all day, yelled at your mom, or stole something; perhaps you bullied some-one or watched someone get bullied. Add these to a new list.

A Message to Me

Now spend the next 45 minutes writing a mes-sage to yourself in 10 years. Tell your future self how you hope you used or did not use your values. Tell yourself the things that you hope you learned from your values. You can also in-clude the things you wished to avoid as you matured.

Ask the group: What did you learn about who you are from this exercise?

Materials:
- Paper
- Pens/pencils

Wrap Up
Explain: Our values are like the bea-cons in a lighthouse or a compass in the desert. They help guide us in the right direction; they help us to know who we are and who we want to be. Use them as you continue to build your understanding of who you are and where you fit in the world.

"If you don't know where you're going, you might not get there."

~Yogi Berra

Learning Goals

Readers will learn to:

1. Understand the importance of planning for the future.
2. Know how to build a plan.

Guiding Questions

How will you navigate life? What's your plan?

From the Book

Chapter	Page Number	How will you navigate life? What's your plan?
17	119	This chapter discusses the need to develop a very specific and detailed plan for your life, with concrete goals to work towards. This model can be used anywhere in the world and at any time. It's never too late to develop a life plan. The chapter talks about plans such as clear educational goals, like learning different languages and developing a book list. Everyone needs a life plan, whether rich or poor, Black or white, in jail or on the streets. Having a life plan is essential for us all.

Release
Life Plan

Tell the group: As Malik traversed the threats of being a drug dealer to the opportunities he found in freedom, he learned a valuable lesson. He needed a plan. Sometimes his plans were rooted in false ideas of what he envisioned success to look like, but for the most part, his plans considered options, analyzed his strengths and weaknesses, and included clear steps to get him from point A (his life as a poor kid) to point B (his life as a free man).

Explain: Our next set of activities will allow you to begin creating a life plan that guides how you navigate your journey from where you are today to where you see yourself in three, five, even ten years from now. You will begin to visualize yourself as you want to be and set goals to achieve that vision.

Activity 1: Doing (120+ mins)
Explain: We need to have a vision for ourselves and our futures. The vision we create for ourselves can help to drive our actions towards attaining success. You will find poster board, magazines, and art supplies on the table. Spend the next two hours creating a vision board that shows where and how you see yourself in three years. Where do you live? What do you do? What makes you happy? What do you want to achieve?

Tell the group: A life plan is just that, a specific plan for your life. It is your "action plan."

It provides a foundation for decision making and standards by which to live. A life plan consists of many elements, such as a personal statement, an assessment of strengths and weaknesses, short- and long-term goals, and several other tools that you will use to achieve and succeed. There are five essential parts of your life plan. See handout.

Give each person a copy of the Life Plan Workbook located at the back of this study guide. You can have them complete it independently or in guided sessions.

After they have completed the Life Plan Workbook, revisit the five areas of a life plan and use the following as a guide for how to wrap up the activity.

Materials:
- Handouts
- Pens/pencils
- Life Plan workbooks

Wrap Up
Explain: A life plan changes as you grow and change. It is something you should revisit at least once a year to see if you're on track for meeting your goals, or if any of your goals have changed because the things you value shifted. Keep a copy of your plan and vision board where you can see them, and review them as often as you can.

Sample Handout

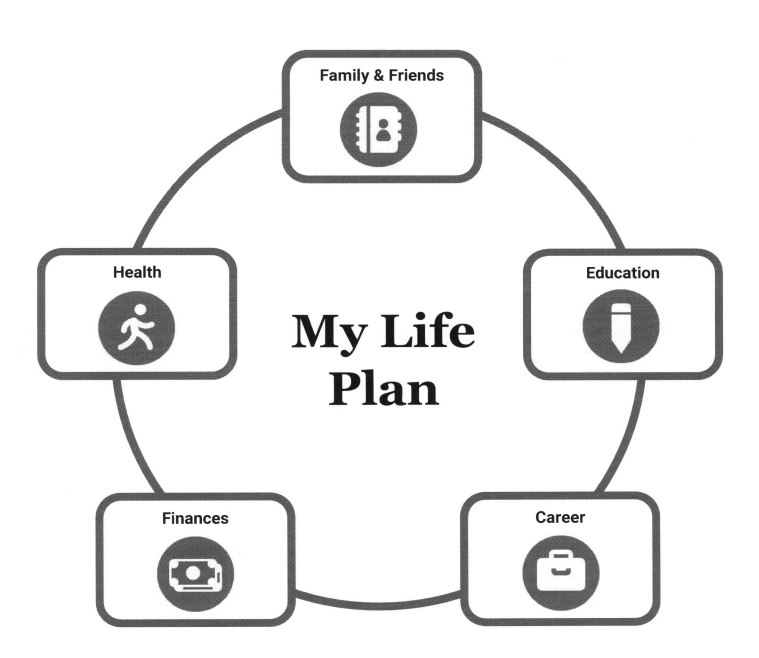

Family & Friends

Health

My Life
Plan

Education

Finances

Career

Release

Transformation

"You were born with potential. You were born with goodness and trust. You were born with ideals and dreams. You were born with greatness. You were born with wings. You are not meant for crawling, so don't. You have wings. Learn to use them and fly."
~ Jalaluddin Mevlana Rumi

Learning Goals

Readers will learn:

1. To understand what personal change and transformation can look like and how to become the person they want to be in the world.
2. About social-emotional development and how it impacts them.

Guiding Question

Who do I want to be?

From the Book

Chapter	Page Number	Who do I want to be?
1	11	In the first paragraph, Malik says, "My drug dealing career started at the age of fifteen when I was growing up in San Francisco." This is the proverbial first stage of the butterfly. Malik is a young egg that will eventually change and transform. Malik makes poor decisions, creates poor relationships, and is unsure of who he is. He is changing but possesses poor social-emotional skills.
15	107	Malik tells us, "Over time I started to learn some very valuable lessons from my prison experience, such as sacrifice, patience, and humility." This passage is important because learning these things precipitated his metamorphosis and evolution into a caterpillar (or a pupa), the two stages where the caterpillar eats and grows rapidly. In Malik's case, he "ate" books, knowledge, and information and grew intellectually. He is also developing his social-emotional skills.
32	241	In this chapter, Malik gets off of parole and has no restrictions. He is now a *butterfly* that can *soar* and fly above anything that previously had been able to restrict him or his movements. He is refining his social-emotional skills.

Tell the group: We all experience changes in our lives. Changes help us grow and become the people we want to be in this world. In the book, we see Malik go through several changes or transformations. He starts as a kid who wants to help his family survive. He becomes a drug dealer who rises to power by being savvy and sometimes savage. By the end of his narrative, he is transformed into a man who knows his path, seeks redemption, and attempts to ensure that other young men do not end up in the cycle of the prison industrial complex that eats so many young people. We will spend the next couple of exercises exploring ideas about who we want to be and learning more about change and transformation as a way to become that person.

Explain: Let's think about a butterfly. A butterfly goes through several stages of development before it becomes the beautiful winged creature we adore. Each stage of its transformation from egg to butterfly serves a purpose and allows it to develop and grow into a monarch or swallowtail. We, like butterflies, go through stages of development that enable us to transform into adults who understand our place in the world.

Release
Transformation

Social and emotional learning deals with how people learn how to engage with others and build skills they need to:

Identify and manage their emotions
Show empathy and respect for others
Build healthy, positive relationships
Solve problems constructively and make good decisions
Navigate stressful or challenging situations

Self-awareness:
Being able to recognize your own emotions, values, strengths, and challenges

Self-management:
Being able to handle your emotions, control impulses, and manage stress to achieve your goals

Responsible decision making:
Being able to make constructive, safe, ethical decisions, both personally and in social situations

Social & emotional learning

Social awareness:
Being able to put yourself in others' shoes and appreciate diverse perspectives

Relationship skills:
Being able to form healthy relationships, work as part of a team, and deal effectively with conflict

> Sample Handout

Self-Awareness includes:
    Recognizing and naming emotions
    Accurate view of yourself
    Identifying strengths, needs, and values
    Belief in yourself
Self-Management involves:
    Managing stress
    Controlling impulses
    Motivating and disciplining yourself
    Setting goals
    Organizational skills
Social Awareness requires:
    Taking someone else's perspective
    Empathy
    Recognizing and appreciating differences
    Showing respect for others
Relationship Skills take:
    Clear communication
    Social engagement and relationship building
    Working cooperatively with others
    Negotiating fairly
    Managing conflicts constructively
    Seeking help
Responsible Decision Making entails:
    Identifying the problem
    Analyzing the situation
    Evaluating solutions
    Reflecting on results
    Making ethical choices
    Responsibility to yourself and others

Release

Transformation

Ask the group: What social-emotional skills have you developed? How do you use them?

Activity 1: Thinking (20 mins)

Tell the group: You will use the wheel in the handout to identify the skills you believe you possess. Once you have thought about them and identified them, check them off on the list on the other handout. It's okay if you don't have them all yet because most of us are refining them as we grow, and even adults sometimes must learn them if they did not learn them as kids. Take Malik. He had to learn some of these social-emotional skills after his incarceration. As a teenager just beginning his life in the world of drugs, he was still in the process of learning some of these lessons. He received the wrong cues as he delved further into a life of crime. It helps to know where you are in the cycle of social-emotional development. You need to know your stages of becoming a butterfly and finding your wings.

Understanding your social-emotional development will help you adapt to change. It will assist you as you transform from the person you are to the person you want to be. It will allow you to handle tough situations and build strong, healthy relationships to support your growth and help you achieve your goals.

Materials:
- Handouts
- Pens/pencils

Take 15 minutes to talk about how they know they reached that stage of the social-emotional cycle.

Activity 2: Doing (60 - 90 mins)

Tell the group: A part of making good transitions in life is knowing where you want to be. It involves holding a vision for your life in front of you at all times. One way to do that is by making a vision board. Vision boards allow us to map how we see our future selves. We can show things like how we look, where we live, what we do, the people we want around us, the things we're passionate about, and how we want to get there.

Show sample vision boards.

Explain: We will now create our vision boards. Use the materials here to build a vision of who you want to be in four years. Be as detailed as possible. You can cut out pictures, draw, use words, and include decorations for emphasis. Tell the story of the future you.

Materials:
- Poster boards
- Markers
- Magazines
- Glue/Paste
- Glitter
- Felt strips

- Crayons
- Paint
- Art supplies

At the end of the hour, bring the group back together and ask them to share their boards and stories.

Wrap Up

Explain: Take your vision board home and put it in a place where you can see it every day. Start taking steps to achieve the vision you created for yourself. Remember that the way to attain the vision is to learn and use your social-emotional skills.

Release

Conclusion

"A wise man learns from the mistakes of others" ~ *Malik Wade*

Conclusion

After such a long and turbulent journey through life with lots of missteps along the way, I thought it was essential to reflect on my past mistakes and develop something that could help others. I decided to write a guide. This lesson study guide accompanies the book that I wrote, *Pressure: From FBI Fugitive to Freedom.*

It was designed to teach individuals (particularly young people) how to think critically and how to evaluate things and see things from a different perspective, using my life as an objective lens. While studying this guide, students are given the opportunity to vicariously insert themselves into my life as an avatar of sorts (without the guru or godlike association). It is my wish that by completing the activities and participating in the discussions that were posed in the lesson plan, readers and participants were able to extract a few life lessons in pragmatic, bite-size chunks that were easy to comprehend. These lessons are based in lived experiences, which make for more authentic learning.

If read and studied carefully, readers will uncover different areas of their lives. This is my small contribution to the body of knowledge in the world. I hope that it serves the reader well and is something that can be studied continuously, similar to any other comprehensive body of work or book that was written and developed to help and heal others.

I would like to end with a quote that is very profound to me and is one of the rules that I live my life by today.

"I want to be remembered as someone who was sincere. Even if I made mistakes, they were made in sincerity. If I was wrong, I was wrong in sincerity."

~ *Malcom X*

Handouts

Steps to Good Decision Making

STEP 1: Analyze

You are confronted with a problem and need to choose how to address it. It may be as simple as what to wear today or as complex as whether or not you, like Malik, would sell drugs or engage in another activity that could compromise your freedom. Before we make the decision or choose which path to take, we must fully understand the problem. We must gather information that helps us see what is at stake.

The first step in our decision-making process is to understand and analyze the problem we face. We must ask ourselves critical questions. What do I need? What do I want? Who will be affected? What is at stake for me? What can I gain? What can I lose? What is most important? How long will it take? These are some of the questions we pose if we are to understand the scope of the problem.

STEP 2: Explore

The next step is to explore our options and weigh the pros and cons of those options. We must consider the potential outcomes of wearing sneakers as opposed to shoes or of selling drugs or not selling them. We must consider the consequences of the possible choices. For example, if I decide to skip class today, I will probably miss valuable information, and I may get called to the principal's office, get detention, or even get a suspension. My decision to skip class can also lead to me getting a poor grade, and that could mean I will have to go to credit recovery. If I decide to not go to work today, I may miss opportunities, I may get written up by my supervisor, or I may even lose my job. Every decision we make has consequences, and we must weigh the cons against the pros to see what will benefit us in the long term.

STEP 3: Decide

The final step is to make a decision. All of this can take place in an instant or over the course of hours, days, or even weeks or months. Some decisions can change the course of our lives forever. Malik's decision to sell drugs, though motivated by the desire to provide for his family, meant he put his freedom at risk and ultimately lost it as a result of this decision. When we decide, when we choose, we owe it to ourselves to do so with information and conviction because some decisions cannot be undone.

Restorative Justice Worksheet

I'm sorry for when I...	Who did my actions hurt? (Myself, my family, my friends, my community?)	How were my actions hurtful?

The Steps to Achieving Restorative Justice

 Recognize that you have done wrong. Before you can apologize for the harm you caused, you must admit to yourself and others that you hurt them in some way. You have to acknowledge the things you did without making excuses for why you did them.

 Issue an apology and seek forgiveness. Once you have admitted the wrong you have done and the harm you have caused, you must find a way to apologize. You can also ask those you have harmed to forgive you for what you have done to them. Your apology can take many forms. Malik wrote a letter; every apology is different, but all apologies should be three things.

3 THINGS EVERY APOLOGY SHOULD BE

1
Sincere: Make it come from the heart. Take time to think about it. Get clear on what you want to say and how you want to say it.

2
Direct: Don't be passive-aggressive. Address those whom you have harmed.

3
Specific: Address specific situations and instances, and be clear about the reasons you are remorseful for your actions or words.

 **Demonstrate through actions that you are sorry.** The final step speaks to making restitution for the things you have done. This too can take many forms. You could fix the things you broke or volunteer at a place representative of the person or place you harmed (for example, a senior center or a youth organization). You could pay for the things you stole or broke. The key to real restorative justice is making things right with yourself and those impacted by your words/actions and also changing your behavior.

Source:"5 Ways To Communicate As Efficiently As A Computer | Fox News." I N.p., n.d. Web. 22 Feb. 2018 <http://www.foxnews.com/us/2016/05/10/5-ways-to-communicate-as-efficiently-as-com>.

A time I felt stressed was when	Thoughts I had about this situation were	I dealt with the feelings by
A time I felt depressed was when	Thoughts I had about this situation were	I dealt with the feelings by
A time I felt happy was when	Thoughts I had about this situation were	I dealt with the feelings by
A time I felt sad was when	Thoughts I had about this situation were	I dealt with the feelings by
A time I felt overwhelmed was when	Thoughts I had about this situation were	I dealt with the feelings by

Coping Strategies

Things I can do when I feel:

Sad

1.

2.

3.

I can talk to

I can go to

Stressed

1.

2.

3.

I can talk to

I can go to

Depressed

1.

2.

3.

I can talk to

I can go to

Overwhelmed

1.

2.

3.

I can talk to

I can go to

Angry

1.

2.

3.

I can talk to

I can go to

Confused

1.

2.

3.

I can talk to

I can go to

Pride vs. Humility

PRIDE	HUMILITY
Knows it all	Seeks to learn
Does it alone	Asks for help
Talks to hear itself	Listens to understand others
Sees others' differences as problems	Sees others' differences as assets
Judges	Accepts
Criticizes	Compliments
Thinks it is perfect	Knows it is imperfect
Does not see fault in itself	Questions itself
Does not do for others	Assists others in need
Unbendable	Bends
Never apologizes	Always apologizes
Goes off	Sucks it up
Expects recognition	Does not need recognition

Things I Like Doing	Things I Hate Doing	Things at Which I Am an Expert
Dancing	Geometry	Snapchat videos
Reading comics	Reading books	Doodling and drawing
Cooking	Talking in front of people	Making pizza

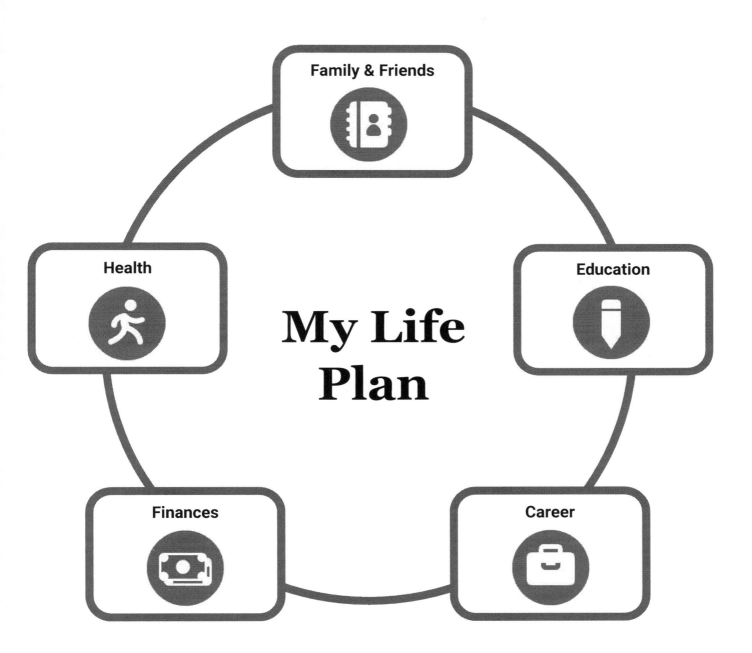

Social and emotional learning deals with how people learn how to engage with others and build skills they need to:

Identify and manage their emotions
Show empathy and respect for others
Build healthy, positive relationships
Solve problems constructively and make good decisions
Navigate stressful or challenging situations

Self-awareness:
Being able to recognize your own emotions, values, strengths, and challenges

Self-management:
Being able to handle your emotions, control impulses, and manage stress to achieve your goals

Responsible decision making:
Being able to make constructive, safe, ethical decisions, both personally and in social situations

Social & emotional learning

Social awareness:
Being able to put yourself in others' shoes and appreciate diverse perspectives

Relationship skills:
Being able to form healthy relationships, work as part of a team, and deal effectively with conflict

Self-Awareness includes:
Recognizing and naming emotions
Accurate view of yourself
Identifying strengths, needs, and values
Belief in yourself
Self-Management involves:
Managing stress
Controlling impulses
Motivating and disciplining yourself
Setting goals
Organizational skills
Social Awareness requires:
Taking someone else's perspective
Empathy
Recognizing and appreciating differences
Showing respect for others
Relationship Skills take:
Clear communication
Social engagement and relationship building
Working cooperatively with others
Negotiating fairly
Managing conflicts constructively
Seeking help
Responsible Decision Making entails:
Identifying the problem
Analyzing the situation
Evaluating solutions
Reflecting on results
Making ethical choices
Responsibility to yourself and others

Life Plan Workbook

Family & Friends

Health

My Life Plan

Education

Finances

Career

Name: _____

Date: _____

Release

Life Plan: Find Your Strengths

Find Your Strengths

Before you start thinking about the five elements of your life plan, take some time to identify what makes you *you*—your strengths, challenges, and unique abilities that will help you achieve your goal. You can start by answering the questions below, but remember that discovering and refining your strengths is a lifelong process. Check in with yourself regularly to think about what you're doing well, what you need help with, and what you'd like to focus on. If you need help identifying your strengths, ask a trusted friend, family member, or teacher.

List what you would consider your top five strengths.

1)

2)

3)

4)

5)

List five areas that you find challenging and would like to improve in.

1)

2)

3)

4)

5)

What is your favorite thing to do in your free time? Why do you enjoy it?

When do you feel at your best? You might think about the time of day, the environment (school, home, the basketball court?), the people around you, or other conditions, such as what you're wearing, what you've had to eat, or how much sleep you've gotten. Include anything you think is important to help you feel your best.

What have people told you you're good at? What's something you're so good at, you could teach someone else how to do it?

What accomplishment are you most proud of? Why?

What's an activity that you enjoy and lose track of time while doing?

What do you like best about yourself?

How would your friends describe you?

Life Plan: Family & Friends

Family and Friends: Your Support System

Your family and friends are the people you spend the most time with, and they form you support system. When you were younger, you may not have thought much about how yo family and friends influenced you, but as you grow up, you'll see how the people around you can help you achieve your goals or make it more difficult to be the person you want t be, depending on their influence. Complete this section of your Life Plan to help you understand yo relationships with family and friends.

Describe your family. Who does it include? Do they live with you, or do they live elsewhere?

Describe your family relationships. Which ones do you value most, and why? Are there any family relationships you'd like to change?

Do you want to live with or near your family in the future? Why or why not?

Do you want to marry? Have children? Why or why not? If you envision starting a family of your own, when do you want that to happen?

Describe your current friendships. Who are your friends? When do you see them, and what do you do together?

What does friendship mean to you? Which friendships do you value most, and why?

Are any of your friendships unhealthy? In what way? How would you like them to change?

Where did you meet your current friends? What opportunities will you have to make new friends in the future (work, school, social groups)?

Do you think your friendships will stay the same or change in the coming years? Why? How will you maintain your friendships?

Release

Life Plan: Education

Education: Shaping Your Future

Malcolm X said, "Education is our passport to the future, for tomorrow belongs only to th people who prepare for it today." You might take school for granted now, but you'll soon have to make your own choices about how you pursue an education. The best way to reac your educational goals is to put together a plan before you finish high school so that life doesn't get in the way of what you want to learn. You don't need to know all the answers now, but it' never too soon to start planning!

What subjects in school do you like best? What are you most excited about learning?

Education doesn't just happen in school. What other ways do you enjoy learning new things?

Describe your current study habits. Do you consider yourself a good student? Why or why not?

What are your educational goals? Do you want to finish high school, attend college or trade school, or pursue a certain certification or training program?

How do you plan to reach your goals? What's your dream school or program? What other options are you considering? How much do they cost?

How long do you think it will take to achieve your educational goals?

How will you pay for school or training? Will you . . .

☐ Apply for scholarships?

☐ Ask family for help?

☐ Use savings?

☐ Work while attending school?

☐ Apply for loans?

☐ Other ideas?

What are the biggest challenges standing between you and your educational goals? Brainstorm ways to overcome these challenges.

Who will help you reach your educational goals? A counselor, trusted adult, or family member? Where can you go when you need encouragement?

Life Plan: Career

Career: Planning for Success

What do you want to be when you grow up? You've probably heard this question before, but your answer might have changed a lot since you were very young. While there's no deadline for deciding what you want to do for the rest of your life, having goals and a plan can help you get started on the path to a fulfilling career in whatever field (or fields!) you choose. Your educational goals go hand in hand with your career goals, so work on these pieces of your Life Plan together.

Not Sure Where to Start?

Take an online assessment to find careers that interest you. Here are some options:

- https://careerwise.minnstate.edu/careers/clusterSurvey
- https://www.mynextmove.org/explore/ip

Explore More

Find additional career exploration tools at: https://www.mynextmove.org

Research Your Top Career Choices

List three careers that are appealing to you, and research them on the U.S. Department of Labor's CareerOneStop site at http://www.careeronestop.org/. How much education do you need to enter these careers? What's the average salary? What's the outlook?

Career	Education required	Average salary	Outlook

After researching your top career choices, which one do you most want to pursue? Why?

What work experience do you have? It could be from a part-time job, helping at a family business, volunteering, or something else. List the skills you gained, and write down what you liked most and least about your work.

Conduct a Career Informational Interview

Do you know anyone who works in the field you aspire to? If so, ask them to meet with you for 15—30 minutes to talk about their job. Prepare a list of 5—10 questions before your meeting, and take notes while you chat. What did you learn about the career that surprised you? Have your feelings about it changed now that you know more?

Release

Life Plan: Finances

Finances: Managing Dollars With Good Sense

What does money mean to you? Maybe you're still living under someone else's roof, and it's fun to spend your money on the things you want. Or maybe you're responsible for some or all of your own expenses, and you watch your dollars carefully. We all need money to meet our needs and plan for a comfortable future, so learning to manage your money wisely is an essential skill. The questions and activities in this section of your Life Plan will get you thinking about how you spend your money now and in the future.

Who supports you financially now? Will this change in the future? When?

How do you earn money now? Do you:

☐ Have a job?

☐ Get an allowance?

☐ Receive gifts of money on special occasions?

Think about your "money models." Do you know someone who is good with money? Do you know someone who struggles with money?

Do you have a bank account? How about a savings account? If not, make a goal to set these up by a certain date.

Who will help you come up with a financial plan and stay on track?

Explore More

Find out more about managing your money at: http://moneyandstuff.info/teens

Where Does Your Money Go?

Being aware of your spending habits is the first step in creating a budget. Try tracking your spending for a week. Write down every dollar you spend, as well as the money you earned from a part-time job, allowance, or gifts. How did your income compare to your expenses?

How much I think I'll spend this week:

Where did my money go?	How much?
Total expenses:	

Total income -	Total expenses =	Remaining balance

Did you spend more, less, or about the same as your prediction? What did you learn about your spending habits?

Life Plan: Health

Health: Taking Care of Your Body and Mind

What do you need to do to feel your best? The answer is different for everyone, but we all need to take care of our health. Eating a healthy diet and staying active are important, as are making healthy choices with your future in mind. Take some time to brainstorm ways you currently take care of your health, and consider the health-related decisions you'll face as you get older. What healthy habits can you establish now so that your body and mind are ready to take you where you want to go in the future?

How I Take Care of My Body	How I Take Care of My Mind

Do you have any health conditions that you have to manage? Do you know your family's health history?

What makes you feel stressed? How does your body feel when you are under stress?

List your top five ways to manage stress.
1)

2)

3)

4)

5)

My Favorite Healthy Foods

My Favorite Ways to Stay Active

Who can you talk to if you have health-related concerns or questions?

Do you have a plan to avoid unwanted pregnancy and sexually transmitted infections (STIs)?

How do you deal with peer pressure to make unhealthy choices, such as drinking alcohol or using drugs?

Explore More

Find out more about staying healthy:

- https://amaze.org
- http://youngmenshealthsite.org
- https://youngwomenshealth.org
- http://goaskalice.columbia.edu

Life Plan: Personal Statement

Personal Statement

While completing this workbook, you've done a lot of thinking about who you are and where you want to go. Now it's time to put it all together.

Start by writing down a brief personal statement to guide your future endeavors. You might have heard of businesses having mission statements. Your personal statement is similar—the idea is that it will help you stay aligned to your values and focused on your priorities. Yo can come up with your personal statement by answering the questions below and then using your ar swers to write one or two sentences that briefly sum up who you are and where you want to go.

1) What is most important to you?

2) What do you most want to accomplish in your life?

3) What are your greatest talents?

4) What do you want people to think about you?

5) When you're gone, what do you want people to remember about you?

My Personal Statement

Setting SMART Goals

Think of the last time you set a goal you didn't reach. Maybe it was to make a ton of money over summer break, or to get an A on your history test. Why were these goals so hard to reach? One reason is that they aren't SMART.

SMART goals are:

- **Specific.** This means they're clear and spelled out in detail.

- **Measurable.** You'll know if you're making progress and can tell when you reach your goal.

- **Achievable.** Was your goal to make $1 million selling your old clothes and shoes? That's probably not something you can accomplish. Achievable goals are realistic.

- **Relevant.** The goal fits into your overall Life Plan.

- **Time-bound.** You have a certain window of time—maybe a week, a month, or a year—in which to achieve the goal.

Let's revisit one of our examples above and make it SMART. Instead of saying, "I want to make a ton of money over summer break," you could say, "My goal is to earn $800 over the 12-week summer break by getting a job at the local ice cream shop, where I'll get paid $8.00 per hour. I'll have to work at least 8.5 hours per week to reach my goal."

Try writing a SMART goal below, and think about SMART goals when writing your Life Plan.

My Goal:

Is my goal . . .

☐ Specific?   ☐ Measurable?   ☐ Achievable?   ☐ Relevant?   ☐ Time-bound?

Writing Your 3-, 5-, and 10-Year Life Plans

When you started this workbook, you might have thought writing a Life Plan would be incredibly difficult, maybe even impossible. But by thinking about the five elements of your Life Plan one by one—family and friends, education, career, finances, and health—you're ready to start planning!

On the following pages, you'll fill in your Life Plans. Where do you want to be in each area of your life in the next 3, 5, and 10 years?

Sometimes a Life Plan feels like a big commitment, but remember that it's *your* life, and you can always change your plan. The important thing is to stay true to yourself, and not to lose sight of your dreams and goals. Review your Life Plan often, especially when you need to make a big decision about your future. Not everything will go according to plan, but if you check in with yourself and make choices that align with your plan, you can live your best life!

Life Plan: My 3-Year Plan

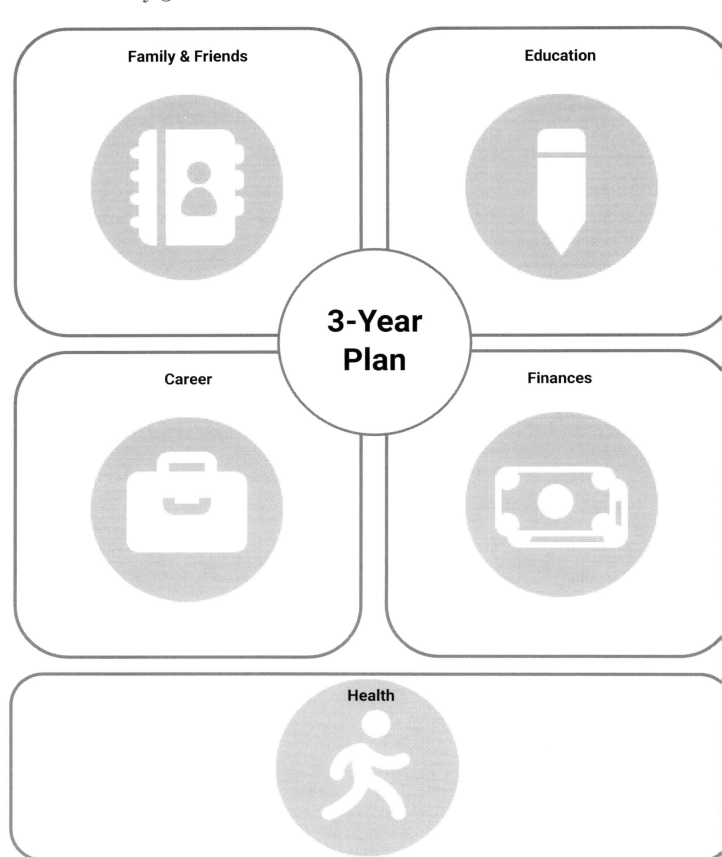

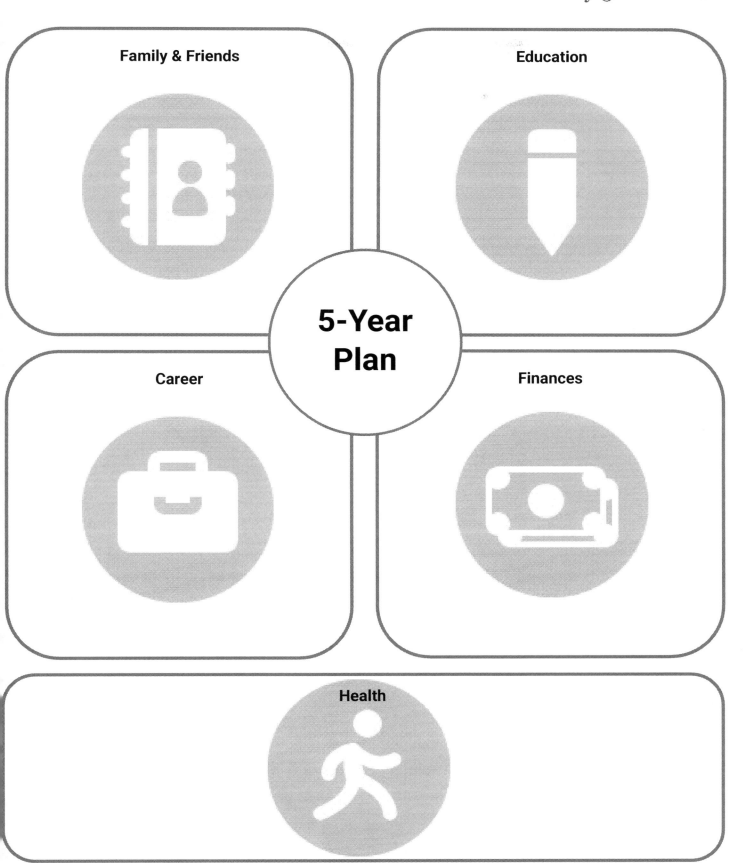

Family & Friends

Education

5-Year Plan

Career

Finances

Health

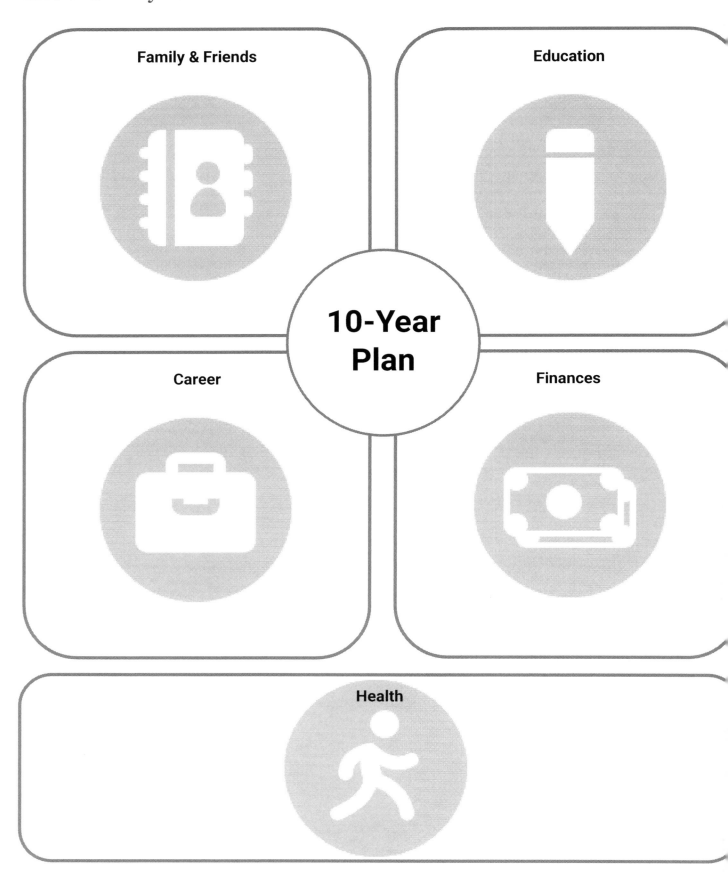

Family & Friends

Education

10-Year Plan

Career

Finances

Health

References

"Asking For Money - Movie Clip from Cinderella Man." *WingClips*, Wing Clips, 2007, www.wingclips.com/movie-clips/cinderella-man/asking-for-money. A movie clip that shows the lead character in the act of being humble.

Cassidy Friedman. "Restorative Justice in a Nutshell." *YouTube*, YouTube, 17 Jan. 2013, www.youtube.com/watch?v=kfmdAJ_eNjE. A short video that describes the restorative justice process.

Ferriman, Justin, and Laura Lynch. "7 Major Learning Styles - Which One Are You?" *LearnDash*, Learn Dash, 21 May 2013, www.learndash.com/7-major-learning-styles-which-one-is-you/. Learning styles used in classroom are described.

Malatesta, Melissa. "The Words." *Pinterest*, 12 Jan. 2014, www.pinterest.com/pin/191121577910584742. Used to create the Pride vs. Humility chart.

Mamas, Michael. "5 Ways to Communicate as Efficiently as a Computer." *Fox News*, FOX News Network, 10 May 2016, www.foxnews.com/us/2016/05/10/5-ways-to-communicate-as-efficiently-as-computer.html. Describes communication skills.

Unknown. "CONCEPTS USED BY PAULO FREIRE." *Freire Institute*, Freire Institute, 1 Feb. 2018, http://www.freire.org/paulo-freire/concepts-used-by-paulo-freire. Describes the concepts used in Freire's work with a definition of conscientization.

Unknown. "Interested in Becoming a Mental-Health Friendly Classroom?" *Classroom Mental Health*, Jan. 2016, classroommentalhealth.org/. Discusses the behavioral health model associated with thoughts, feelings, and behaviors experienced by students.

CASEL. "Social and Emotional Learning (SEL) Competencies." Collaborative for Academic, Social, and Emotional Learning, January 2017, https://casel.org/wp-content/uploads/2017/01/Competencies.pdf. Describes and gives context to social-emotional learning.

Made in the USA
Middletown, DE
03 October 2020